THE LÉVITIKON:

THE GOSPELS ACCORDING TO
THE PRIMITIVE CHURCH

The Lévitikon
Apostolic Johannite Church
www.johannite.org

Translated from the French
by The Rev. Deacon Donald J. Donato

.

    ISBN   978-1-894981-99-6
    1. Gnosticism–Miscellanea
I. Title

Printed and bound in the United States

THE LÉVITIKON:

THE GOSPELS ACCORDING TO
THE PRIMITIVE CHURCH

FROM THE THRONE OF ST. JOHN

Dear Friends,

The publication of *The Lévitikon: The Gospels According to the Primitive Church* represents the combined efforts of many talented clergy and laity. Yet, not only does it represent their efforts but also their spirit, one of dedication and love to the Johannite Tradition and the Church which stands foremost among those who serve it, the Apostolic Johannite Church.

From His Grace the Primate of Spain to the Reverend Donald Donato and the Apostolic Council of the Apostolic Johannite Church, as well as many other people who laboured behind the scenes to make this work available- each one has dedicated not only their time and energy but their very lives to the task of upholding and living that same tradition.

Nor are these efforts limited to those who are with us now, but also those who have tread the path before us- and with this publication, the Apostolic Johannite Church seeks to honour its spiritual predecessors in the work of the Johannite Tradition, the L'Eglise Johannites des Primitif Chretiens more accurately known as L'Eglise Chretienne, headed by its Sovereign Pontiff and Patriarch, ‡BERNARDUS RAYMONDUS, Bernard-Raymond Fabré-Palaprat.

More than any single figure in modern Gnostic and Esoteric history, Bernard-Raymond Fabré-Palaprat worked to make the Johannite Tradition more than just a one-among-many, attempting to secure its place as a tradition to be lived, worked and continued as a distinct entity, rather than simply to be celebrated on the feasts of the Holy Saints John alone.

It is this work that the Apostolic Johannite Church takes up and continues, not for the sake of claiming a sole command over a lineage that is the common heritage of all Gnostic Churches, but for the sake of the living power of the tradition itself. We know, as he knew, that this Tradition is too precious of a jewel to be relegated to a secondary status, where it risks merely adorning the walls of its clerics rather than furnishing the hearts and minds of its adherents

Thus, *The Lévitikon: The Gospels According to the Primitive Church* represents a powerful moment in the history of both the Apostolic Johannite Church and the Johannite tradition.

For the Apostolic Johannite Church, it represents our continuing commitment to our Statement of Principles–freedom of spiritual exploration, accessible to all, nurturing to individual expression and wider community alike. The Apostolic Johannite Church works to consistently follow its principles in all that it does–and with the act of bringing to you a pivotal text of the Ecclesiastical Gnostic movement for study and spiritual reflection, it continues this direction in the present day.

For the Johannite tradition, this text represents more than a mere historical curiosity, it is a kind of anamnesis recalling the spirit and dedication of all those who so dedicated their lives to the real meaning of what it means to be a Johannite: the commandment to love one another, which is directed at every seeker–be they pilgrim or Pontiff.

Ultimately, it is my hope that you will, as I have, through the course of exploring this text, grow in understanding and harmony with that same meaning and dedication. It is my prayer for you that it may lead to a more complete communion with the Divine in yourself through the person of your fellow seekers.

Given in Calgary, at the Oratory of St. John the Beloved, on May 23rd, the Feast of Pentecost, in the Two-Thousandth and Tenth year of Our Lord, the seventh of my Patriarchate.

‡IOHANNES IV
Sovereign Pontiff and Patriarch

THE LÉVITIKON

The story has it that in 1804–the year Napoleon became Emperor and Thomas Jefferson became president–a young French doctor named Bernard-Raymond Fabré-Palaprat (1777-1838) found, in a Paris bookseller's cart, an ancient manuscript, reportedly medieval. The brief preface to the text claimed to have been penned by one Nicephorus of Athens, a monk. The document, in Greek, was for the most part a common copy of the *Gospel of John*.

For the most part.

There are certain critical additions to and omissions from the conventional telling. It ends at the Nineteenth Gospel and not the Twenty First (neglecting to include any resurrection narrative). It is not merely incomplete; it deliberately concludes with the entombment of Jesus, a teaching about the remission of sins usually found in the Twentieth Gospel, and this resolution:

> John the Disciple that Jesus loved gives
> testimony to the truth of this scripture so
> that you believe it, and so that you will
> teach it.

There are other interesting additions. In the Sixth Gospel, when the Jews question Jesus' claims to have come down from heaven, the customary confusion is that his parents are known to the crowd: "Do we not know his mother and father?" However, in this curious text, the question is posed;

9

Is it because he lived with the Greeks
that he has come thus to converse with
us?   What is there in common with what
he learned from the Egyptians, and that
which our fathers taught us?

This presents Jesus as a bearer of alien information –he carries with him a source of teachings outside of *Torah*. This portrayal of Jesus as outsider, misunderstood by his ambient culture, becomes critical later on, and characterizes the entire Gospel.

Of specific note, and the hinge to the whole affair, is this peculiar passage inserted at the end of the Seventeenth Gospel;

10

In truth, I say unto you that I am not of
this world, but John will be your father
until he comes to be with me in Paradise,
and he will anoint in the Holy Spirit.

John will be your father. Not Peter. John. This purportedly authentic medieval manuscript claims that Jesus was an initiate of secret Egyptian teachings, unknown to the Church of St. Peter, and that these teachings were preserved by the Church of St. John – the Johannites.

THE GOSPEL OF JOHN

Now the people were filled with
expectation, and all were asking in their
hearts whether John [the Baptist] might be
the Messiah. – Luke 3:15

The Gospel of John is both the youngest and oldest of the canonical Gospels.   Almost universally considered to have been composed after the others, it is the first for which we have archaeological evidence (around 130 CE); and the community of authorship pre-dates the ministry of Jesus. So, although the most recently composed, it has the most ancient pedigree.

John is enticingly out of step with the synoptic Gospels of Matthew, Mark and Luke. Its theology is more subtle, and more sublime.

John omits Jesus' virgin birth of the synoptic stories, as well as the term "apostle" – but it deals frequently on "otherness"; the community's distinction from Judaism, from "the world", from other Christians. Its Platonist introduction and high Christology casts John as less a history than an architecture of ideas: Christ as *Logos*–not merely "word" but in the Greek understanding of "ideal"; the essential *rightness* of things. Also of significance is that Mary Magdalene plays a more prominent role, and she among all of Jesus' followers visits his tomb alone.

The only "John" in the *Gospel of John* is John the Baptist; the identification of "the disciple whom Jesus loved" with John the Evangelist is largely discounted by biblical scholars. *John* is the Gospel –more technically Gospels–of a community comprised initially of the the followers of John the Baptist, some of whom rejected the divinity of Jesus as others accepted it.

Biblical scholar Raymond Brown, author of the critical *Community of the Beloved Disciple*, sees the development of *John* in four Phases; the first involved the community emerging and distinguishing itself from first century Judaism to the extent that it was expelled from the Temple. The second deals

11

with the group's members coming to terms with their new distinct identity, and their view of "the Jews" as antagonistic outsiders. The third phase details a rift between the more esoteric-minded of the community (the eventual "secessionists") and those subscribing to what we later identify as orthodoxy. The fourth phase sees the disintegration of communion, with the secessionists leaving the orthodox to pursue Gnosticism; a fairly natural evolution of thought. As Brown states:

> "A savior who came from an alien world above, who said that neither he nor those who accepted him were of this world, and who promised to return to take them to a heavenly dwelling could be fitted into the gnostic world picture."

> "This explains why the Fourth Gospel, which they brought with them, is cited earlier and more frequently by heterodox writers than by orthodox writers.... If the Johannine eagle soared above the earth, it did so with talons bared for the fight; and the last writings that were left show the eaglets tearing at each other for the possession of the nest."

It is these Gnostics, with their history and Gospel rooted in the community of the "disciple whom Jesus loved" who leave a fascinating and enduring thread through the tapestry of western religion–a thread which through fate, inheritance or forgery (or perhaps a combination of all three) Fabré-Palaprat was centuries later to take up.

So we have the initiation-rite community around John the Baptist which along with The Twelve comprises the kernel of the "Jesus Movement", and then a distinct sect-identity as "the community of the Beloved Disciple". This community suffers a schism, with the majority leaving the sect in favour of a more Platonist, esoteric framework and adopting what we later understand as Gnosticism. These Gnostics spawn numerous communities, considering themselves privy to authentic source teachings not available to those outside the movement. The Valentinian Gnostics were heavily Johannite in their theology and practice, and Valentinus' own student Heracleon produced the very first Gospel commentary (on *John*).

THE ORDER OF THE TEMPLE

We know these movements existed, as they exist today in surviving groups such as the Mandaeans. However, *The Levitikon* hinted at something far more exotic – a ligature between surviving Johannite communities and the Knights Templar. With what can only be considered little more than legend, Templar Grand Master Hughes de Payens is invested with the Patriarchate of the Church of St. John, along with Apostolic Succession, by one Theoclete. Further, the legend has the Templar Order surviving the massacre of Templars in 1314 through the transfer of legitimate Grand Mastery (via the dubious *Charter* of 1324) to a certain Larmenius, who in turn invests both Templar and Johannite authority to Prior Franciscus Theobaldus in Alexandra, and on over the hoary centuries to the good doctor, Fabré-Palaprat.

'Up to the year 1118 the mysteries and the hierarchic Order of the initiation of Egypt,

transmitted to the Jews by Moses,
then to the Christians by Jesus Christ,
were preserved by the successors of St.
John. These mysteries and initiations
... were a sacred trust ... preserved from
all adulteration ... These Christians,
appreciating the courage and piety of the
[Templar] Crusaders ... held it their duty
to trust to hands so pure the knowledge
acquired over so many centuries. ...
Hugues de Payens (the Templar Grand
Master) was invested with the Apostolic
Patriarchal Power and placed in the
legitimate order of the successors of St.
John...

'Such is the origin of the foundation of
the Order of the Temple and of the fusion
in this Order of the different kinds of
initiation ... designated under the title of
Primitive Christians or Johannites.'
    – *Manuel des Chevaliers du Temple (1811)*

Thus, Fabré-Palaprat reconstituted both the Order of the Temple and the Primitive Christian Church of St. John, organized and illustrated through the vessel of nineteenth century Freemasonry. Assisting the doctor was the Monsignor Mauviel, a Haitian bishop consecrated in 1800, who bestowed both ecclesiastical legitimacy and Apostolic Succession upon this resuscitated venture. Regardless of the questionability of the source documents, the Johannite Church was a real, legitimate ecclesiastical undertaking with valid sacraments and sincere seekers.

POSSIBILITIES

1) The entire enterprise was a fraud perpetrated by Fabré-Palaprat, and the document a forgery concocted to provide his occult society with authority.

2) The document is a modern forgery, and Fabré-Palaprat unwittingly "fell for" what amounts to a practical joke. One wonders what the motive would be, however. Now, we do see a number of Enlightenment era attempts to euhemerize the bible through aggressive redaction; but these tend to omit any miraculous events. In contrast the *Lévitikon's John* includes the miracles of the loaves and fishes, water into wine, and the raising of Lazarus.

3) *The Lévitikon* is an authentic medieval document, but its authorship was spontaneous; which is to say that someone originated this version *ex nihilo* in the 12th century.

4) The document is authentic and genuinely speaks to an existing tradition or legends concerning the Gospels, but was only written down when this text was penned.

5) The document is an accurate copy of much older text, and is in effect an alternate accounting of the Gospel of John, before later and more familiar redactions.

Regardless of which assumption one chooses, *The Lévitikon* stands on its own merits in one vital regard; it is an interesting opportunity for reframing the question of the Gospels and authority. In a milieu of post-Revolutionary anti-clericalism, the Johannite Church was an attempt at reframing the bible through a lens outside of the Catholic/

Protestant dyad. Authentic valid, and historical, but outside of the troublesome associations of the See of Peter. It offered a way of reaching back to "primitive" authority as a kind of end-run around the Papacy without resorting to Puritanism or Calvinism, which would have had little appeal to Fabré-Palaprat's aesthetic of Napoleonic grandeur and the remaking of Europe in the Imperial image. Even were the entire thing counterfeit, it would be no less significant than that other ecclesiastical forgery, *The Donation of Constantine*, which resulted in the assumption of the Roman Empire by the Papacy.

What are we left with? Questionable half-histories, redacted gospels, myth and legend. But at the same time, we have communities of tradition, inquiry, and service. The entire Johannite continuum, of saints and scoundrels both, smacks of *sensus plenior* – a kind of divine significance unimagined by the milieu and egos of the architects. The Johannite Church stands today in a balance of alternative and continuity, of ancient liturgy and innovative inquiry. Holding ideas of Gnostic heresy and Christian orthodoxy in dynamic tension, it manifests weekly in traditional Eucharists, and daily in pastoral phone calls, hospital and prison visits, and academic research.

It is in this context of service, inquiry and inspiration that we bring to you the first English translation of *The Gospels According to the Primitive Church*.

The Very Rev. Monsignor Jordan Stratford STL
Prefect for the Congregation on Ecumenical Relations
& Apostolic Prefect for British Columbia

THE LÉVITIKON:

THE GOSPELS ACCORDING TO THE PRIMITIVE CHURCH

*Originally published
by The Most Rev. ✠Bernard-Raymond
Fabré-Palaprat,
Sovereign Pontiff and Patriarch of the
Johannite Church*

*Translated by
The Rev. Deacon Donald J. Donato*

Historical note on the original publisher:
Another book published by "A. Guyuot et Scribe" appears as a recent acquisition of the Loyola Marymount University Library, Special Collection, row 28, call number QB803 .S45 1817. This is a reference to a book on Astronomy given by the Charles Boyer Collection in 1963 to the Record Commission in the United Kingdom of Great Britain and Northern Ireland. The volume was dated 1834. In this catalogue reference, the Paris-based publisher is listed as "A. Guyot et Scribe, Printers to the King," not "Printer" (sing.) as in this edition of Lévitikon Great Seal of the Government of the Christian Church.[1]

18

A. Guyot, Printer to the King,
Rue Neuve-des-Petits-Champs, No. 37.

LÉVITIKON

Or an exposé of the fundamental principles of the doctrines of the primitive, catholic Christians, following their gospels, an extract from the Golden Table (tablet), and the ceremonial ritual of their religious services, etc., and preceded by the Statute on the Government of the Church and the levitical hierarchy.

DEDICATION

For

OUR LADY AND HER DAUGHTERS
from whom we are born,
and with whom we live, work and celebrate life.

TRANSLATOR'S PREFACE

This work of translation would not have been possible without the kind consideration and patience of the Patriarch and Apostolic Council of the Apostolic Johannite Church. Beginning in Strasbourg in the spring of 2008, and ending in Boston only in the spring of 2010, the translation of the Gospels represents a very important part of my formation both into Holy Orders and as a person.

This translation is as literal as possible, with the exception of grammatical constructs that are more appropriate to the English reader. The format is as true to the original as possible. That being the case, there are no numbered verses, and every effort has been made to preserve the stylistic elements of the original French text. Where there is a question of meaning, a comparison with the original Greek has been made. For measures, the denominations used in the original *Lévitikon*, and not common English measures, have been kept intact with explanatory notes on the conversion. Contemporary English with Canadian spelling has been used owing to the location of the Apostolic Johannite Church's Patriarchate in Calgary, Alberta.

When approached from the viewpoint of literary criticism, the Gospel translated here is often simpler and shorter than the version of the *Gospel of John* which appears in other translations. Very often the reader will notice that the messianic references of the canonical gospel, which attempt to link Jesus of Nazareth to ancient Hebrew prophecy, simply do not appear. The same is true of 'miracles', 'wonders' or 'works', at times appearing in the French as the 'science' of Jesus.

This translation owes a special debt of gratitude to the Andover-Harvard Theological Library at Harvard Divinity School in Cambridge, and to the Robert D. Farber University Archives and Special Collections at Brandeis University in Waltham, Massachusetts. The Brandeis Library provided me with an inspirational setting for this work, surrounded by precious copies of Judaic scriptures and the sacred artefacts of Jewish spirituality, rescued from the clutches of ignorance, persecution and the Nazi scourge. St. John the Beloved Disciple and founder of the Secret Church from which the Johannite Tradition flows, was also called "Levi", alternately translated from the Hebrew meaning either "priest" or one who is "joined" to others. In his memory, and for the hundreds of Johannite leaders down through the ages, there can be no doubt that the motto of Brandeis University strikes at the heart of our work: "Truth, even unto its innermost parts." It is a source of joy to know that this work will open up the search for truth in ways that were previously not possible for the English-speaking peoples.

Haec mando vobis ut diligatis invicem.

Reverend Donald J. Donato
Boston, Massachusetts
The Annunciation of Our Lady 2010

PREFACE

The archives of the Apostolic Court exclusively contain the historical documents of the primitive, catholic, Christian Church; we have developed the project of publishing them with the authorization of the Prince of the Apostles and the Court. As much as this exacting work of research from which it seems impossible for the Court to deliver itself at the moment, we still could not exempt ourselves in replying to the just request of the priests who have resolved to declare, at last publicly, the worship of the Church of the Christ.

It is for this reason that we have freed for printing the writings which contain the fundamental principles of the primitive Christian religion which are as indispensible to the ministers as to the faithful.

These manuscripts are principally the *Lévitikon* and the Gospels. Additionally, there is an extract of the *Golden Tablet, the Basic Statute of the Government of the Church, the Ritual Ceremonial of the Religious Service,* etc. We have to recall that the *Lévitikon,* the Gospels and of the extract of the Golden Tablet are from the translation of one of the manuscripts retrieved from the sacred treasure of the Christian Church.

This manuscript is in Greek on parchments (large leaf) in letters of gold, bearing the date of 1154. It is a copy or an apograph of a manuscript from the fifth century, preserved by our brothers in the East, similar to the copy from the West save the passages related to the Order of the Temple which were incorporated by the Primitive Church at its founding in 1118, as well as some notes and passages taken from traditional religious and doctrinal commentary, which the Apostolic Court ordered to be included in all translations of the levitical codex.

24

THE GOSPELS
OF THE
PRINCE OF APOSTLES, SOVEREIGN PONTIFF
AND PATRIARCH JOHN,
CONSECRATED IN THE PRIMITIVE CHURCH

"the Word" beginning of spells ↑A

(Literal Translation)

FIRST GOSPEL

In the beginning was the Word, and the Word was with God, and God was the Word. This one was with God at the beginning. In him was life, and life was the light. And the light shines in the darkness, and darkness did not understand it at all.

It came to pass that God sent a man, who was called John. He came in testimony to render testimony of the light, and so all would believe through him. He was not the light, but was to render testimony of the light.

There was the true light which, coming into the world, enlightens all mankind. He was in the world, and the world was made through him, and the world did not know him. He came to his own, and those who were his own did not receive him. But as many as received him, to them he gave the right to become children of God, even to those who believe in his name, who were born, not of blood nor of the will of the flesh nor of the will of man, but of God.

He was made flesh and lived among us, and we saw his glory; a glory as an only son of a father full of grace and truth. John gave testimony about him and cried out, saying: This was he of whom I said; he who comes after me has a higher rank than I, for he existed before me. For of his fullness we have all received, and grace upon grace, because the Law was given through Moses, and grace and truth were given through Jesus Christ. No one has seen God at any time. The only Son, who is in the breast of the Father, he has explained him.

This is the testimony of John, when the Jews sent to him Priests and the Levites from Jerusalem to ask him: Who are you? And he avowed and did not deny, but avowed: I am not the Christ. They asked him: What then? Are you Elijah? And he said: I am not. Are you the Prophet? And he answered: No. Then they said to him: Who are you, so that we may give an answer to those who sent us? What do you say about yourself? He said: I am a voice of one crying in the wilderness, make straight the way of the Lord, as Isaiah the prophet said.

And those that had been sent from (in the name of) the Pharisees, and they asked him, and said to him: Why then do you baptize, if you are not the Christ, nor Elijah, nor the Prophet? John answered them saying: I baptize in water, but among you stands (one) whom you do not know. It is he who comes after me, the thong of whose sandal I am not worthy to untie. These things took place in Bethany beyond the Jordan, where John was baptizing.

The next day he saw Jesus coming to him and said: Behold, the Lamb of God who takes away the sin of the world. This is he of whom I said: A man comes before me who was made before me because he is first before me. I did not recognize him, but so that he might be manifested to Israel, I came baptizing in water. John testified saying: I have seen the Spirit descending as a dove out of Heaven, and it remained upon him. I did not recognize him, but he who sent me to baptize in water said to me: He upon whom you see the Spirit descending and remaining upon him, this is the one who baptizes in the Holy Spirit. I myself have seen, and have testified that this is the Son of God.

The next day John was standing again with two of his Disciples. And he cast his eyes on Jesus as he walked, and he said: Behold, the Lamb of God. And his Disciples heard him speak, and they followed Jesus. And Jesus turned and saw them following, and said to them: What do you seek? But they said to him: Rabbi, which translated means teacher, where are you staying? He said to them: Come, and you will see. So they came and saw where he was staying; and they stayed with him that day, for it was about the tenth hour. Andrew, the brother of Simon Peter, was one of the two who heard John speak and who had followed him. He found first his own brother Simon and said to him: We have found the Messiah, which means the Christ. He brought him to Jesus. Now Jesus looked at him and said: You are Simon the son of Jonas. You shall be called Peter.

The next day he wanted to go into Galilee, and he found Philip and said to him: Follow me. Now Philip was from Bethsaida, of the city of Andrew and Peter. Philip found Nathanael and said to him: We have found Him of whom Moses in the Law and also the Prophets wrote—Jesus, the son of Joseph of Nazareth. And Nathanael said to him: Can any good thing come out of Nazareth? Philip said to him: Come and see. Jesus saw Nathanael coming to him, and said of him: Here, truly an Israelite, in whom there is no deceit. Nathanael said to him: How do you know me? Jesus answered and said to him: Before Philip called you, I saw you when you were under the fig tree. Nathanael answered him:

Rabbi, you are the Son of God; you are the King of Israel. Jesus answered and said to him: Because I said to you that I saw you under the fig tree, do you believe? You will see greater things than these. And he said to him: In truth, in truth I say to you, you will see Heaven open and the Angels of God ascending and descending on the Son of man.

✳

SECOND GOSPEL

A wedding took place at Cana of Galilee, and the mother of Jesus was there. And both Jesus and his Disciples were also invited. Now, the wine ran out, the mother of Jesus said to him: They do not have any wine at all. There were six stone pots in this place, containing about two or three measures. Jesus said to them: fill the pots with water and bring them closer to me. And they filled them up to the top; and having touched the water, he said to them: You can now carry them to the headwaiter. And they took them to him.

29

When the headwaiter tasted the water which had become wine, and he did not know where it came from. But the servants who had drawn the water knew. The headwaiter called the bridegroom and said to him: Every man serves the good wine first, and when the people have drunk freely; then he serves the poorer wine. But you, you have kept the good wine until now. Jesus had done his first astonishing thing, and manifested his science, and his Disciples believed in him. After this he went down to Capernaum, he and his mother and his brothers and his disciples; and they stayed there a few days.

The Passover of the Jews was near, and Jesus went up to Jerusalem. And he found in the sanctuary those who were selling oxen and sheep and doves, and the money changers seated at their tables. And he reproached them for their impiety, and they left from that place. And he began to preach.

And some of them understood his teachings; believed in his name, but Jesus for his part was not entrusting himself to them, for he knew all men. He knew everything about them and he possessed all the sciences. He did not need anyone to testify concerning man because he himself knew everything there is to know about the outside and the inside of man.

✱
THIRD GOSPEL

Now there was a man of the Pharisees, named
Nicodemus, a ruler of the Jews. This man came to
Jesus by night and said to him: Rabbi, we know that
you have come from God as a teacher; for no one
can do these signs that you do unless God is with
him. Jesus answered and said to him: In truth, in
truth, I say to you, unless one is born from above[2]
he cannot know the kingdom of God. Nicodemus
said to him: How can a man be born when he is old?
He cannot enter a second time into his mother's
womb and be born, can he? Jesus answered: In
truth, in truth, I say to you, unless one is born
of water and the Spirit he cannot enter into the
kingdom of God. That which is born of the flesh is
flesh, and that which is born of the Spirit is spirit.
Do not be astonished that I said to you, 'You must be
born from above.' The wind blows where it wishes
and you hear the sound of it, but do not know where
it comes from and where it is going; so is everyone
who is born of the Spirit.

Nicodemus said to him: How can these things be?
Jesus answered and said to him: Are you the teacher
of Israel and do not understand these things? Truly,
truly, I say to you, we speak of what we know and
testify of what we have seen, and you do not accept
our testimony. If I told you earthly things and you
do not believe, how will you believe if I tell you
heavenly things? No one has ascended into heaven,
but he who descended from heaven: the Son of man.
As Moses lifted up the serpent in the wilderness,
even so must the Son of man be lifted up: so that

whoever believes will in him have eternal life. For God so loved the world, that he gave his only Son, that whoever believes in him shall not perish, but have eternal life. For God did not send the Son into the world to judge the world, but that the world might be saved by him. He who believes in him is not judged; he who does not believe has been judged already, because he has not believed in the name of the only begotten Son of God. This is the judgment, that the Light has come into the world, and men loved the darkness rather than the Light, for their deeds were evil. For everyone who does evil hates the Light, and does not come to the Light for fear that his deeds will be exposed. But he who practices the truth comes to the Light, so that his deeds may be manifested as having been wrought in God.

After these things Jesus and his disciples came into the land of Judea, and there he was spending time with them and baptizing. John also was baptizing in Aenon near Salem, because there was much water there; and people were coming and were being baptized— for John had not yet been thrown into prison. Therefore there arose a discussion on the part of John's Disciples with a Jew about purification. And they came to John and said to him: Rabbi, He who was with you beyond the Jordan, to whom you have testified, behold, He is baptizing and all are coming to Him. John answered and said: A man can receive nothing unless it has been given him from heaven. You yourselves are my witnesses that I said: I am not the Christ, but I have been sent ahead of him. He who has the bride is the bridegroom; but the friend of the bridegroom, who stands and hears him, rejoices greatly because of the bridegroom's voice. So this joy of mine has been made full. He must increase, but I must decrease.

He who comes from above is above all, he who is of the earth is from the earth and speaks of the earth. He who comes from heaven is above all. What he has seen and heard, of that he testifies; and no one receives his testimony. He who has received his testimony has set his seal to this, that God is true. For he whom God has sent speaks the words of God; for he gives the Spirit without measure. The Father loves the Son and has given all things into his hand. He who believes in the Son has eternal life; but he who does not obey the Son will not see life, but the wrath of God abides on him

✳

FOURTH GOSPEL

Therefore when the Lord knew that the Pharisees had heard that Jesus was making and baptizing more Disciples than John, he left Judea and went away again into Galilee. But he had to pass through Samaria (to get to) Sychar, near the parcel of ground that Jacob gave to his son Joseph; and Jacob's well was there. So Jesus, being wearied from his journey, was sitting thus by the well. It was about the sixth hour.

There came a woman of Samaria to draw water. Jesus said to her: Give me a drink. For his disciples had gone away into the city to buy food. And so the Samaritan woman said to him: How is it that you, being a Jew, ask me for a drink when I am a Samaritan woman? For Jews have no dealings with Samaritans. Jesus answered and said to her: If you knew the gift of God, and who it is who says to you, 'Give me a drink,' you would have asked him, and he would have given you living water. She said to him: Sir, you have nothing to draw with and the well is deep; where then do you get that living water? You are not greater than our father Jacob, are you, who gave us the well, and drank of it himself and his sons and his cattle? Jesus answered and said to her: Everyone who drinks of this water will thirst again; but whoever drinks of the water that I will give him shall never thirst; but the water that I will give him will become in him a well of water springing up to eternal life.

The woman said to him: Sir, give me this water, so I will not be thirsty nor come all the way here to draw. He said to her: Go, call your husband and come here. The woman answered and said: I have no husband. Jesus said to her: You have correctly said, 'I have no husband'; for you have had five husbands, and the one whom you now have is not your husband; this you have said truly. The woman said to him: Sir, I see that you are a Prophet. Our fathers worshiped in this mountain, and you people say that Jerusalem is the place where we ought to worship. Jesus said to her: Woman, believe me, an hour is coming when neither in this mountain nor in Jerusalem will you worship the Father. You worship what you do not know; we worship what we know, for salvation[3] is from the (doctrine of the) Jews. But an hour is coming, and now is, when the true worshipers will worship the Father in spirit and truth; for such people the Father seeks to be his worshipers. God is spirit, and those who worship him must worship in spirit and truth. The woman said to him: I know that the Messiah is coming, he who is called Christ; when that one comes, he will call all to him. Jesus said to her: I who speak to you am he.

At this point his Disciples came, and they were astonished that he had been speaking with a woman. Yet no one said: What do you ask? or: Why do you speak with this woman? So the woman left her water pot, and went into the city and said to the men: Come, see a man who told me all the things that I have done; this is not the Christ, is it? They went out of the city, and were coming to him. Meanwhile the Disciples were urging him, saying: Rabbi, eat. But he said to them, I have food to eat that you do not know about. So the Disciples were saying to one another: No one brought him anything to eat, did he? Jesus said to them: My food is to do the will of him who sent me and to accomplish his work. Do you not say: There are yet four months, and then comes the harvest? Behold, I say to you, lift up your eyes and look on the fields, that they are white for harvest. Already he who reaps is receiving wages and is gathering fruit for life eternal; so that he who sows and he who reaps may rejoice together. For in this case the saying is true, 'One sows and another reaps.' I sent you to reap that for which you have not laboured; others have laboured and you have entered into their labour."

From that city many of the Samaritans believed in him because of the word of the woman who testified: He told me all the things that I have done. So when the Samaritans came to Jesus, they were asking him to stay with them; and he stayed there two days. Many more believed because of his word; and they were saying to the woman: It is no longer because of what you said that we believe, for we have heard for ourselves and know that this one is indeed the saviour of the world. After the two days he went forth from there into Galilee. For Jesus himself testified that a prophet has no honour in his own country. So when he came to Galilee, the

Galileans, having seen all the things that he did, received him.

Therefore he came again to Cana of Galilee where he had made the water wine. And there was a military official whose son was sick at Capernaum. When he heard that Jesus had come out of Judea into Galilee, he went to Him and was imploring Him to come down and heal his son; for he was at the point of death. So Jesus said to him: Unless you people see wonders, you will not believe. The military official said to him: Sir, come down before my child dies. Jesus said to him: I go so that your son lives. This is the second sign that Jesus performed.

✳
FIFTH GOSPEL

There was a feast of the Jews, and Jesus went up to Jerusalem. Now there is in Jerusalem, by the Probatic[4], a pool, which is called in Hebrew Bethesda, having five porticoes. In these lay a multitude of those who were sick, blind, lame, and withered, and there was a man was there who had been ill for many days. When Jesus saw him lying there, and knew that he had already been a long time in that condition, he said to him: Do you wish to get well? The sick man answered him: Sir, I have no man to put me into the pool. Jesus said to him: Get up, pick up your cot and walk. Immediately the man became well, and picked up his cot and began to walk.

Now it was the Sabbath on that day. So the Jews were saying to the man who was cured: It is the Sabbath, and it is not permissible for you to carry your cot. But he answered them: He who made me well was the one who said to me: 'Pick up your cot and walk.' They asked him: Who is the man who said to you: 'Pick up your cot and walk'? But the man who was healed did not know who it was, for Jesus had slipped away while there was a crowd in that place. Afterward Jesus found him in the temple and said to him: Behold, you have become well; do not sin anymore, so that nothing worse happens to you. The man went away, and told the Jews that it was Jesus who had made him well. For this reason the Jews were persecuting Jesus, because he was doing these things on the (day of the) Sabbath. But he answered them: My Father is working until now, and I myself am working.

For this reason therefore the Jews were seeking all the more to kill him, because he not only was breaking the Sabbath, but also was calling God his own Father, making himself equal with God. Therefore Jesus answered and was saying to them: In truth, in truth, I say to you, the Son can do nothing of himself, unless it is something he sees the Father doing; for whatever the Father does, these things the Son also does in the same way. For the Father loves the Son, and shows him all things that he himself is doing; and the Father will show him greater works than these, so that you will be astonished. For just as the Father raises the dead and gives them life, even so the Son also gives life to whom he wishes. For not even the Father judges anyone, but he has given all judgment to the Son, so that all will honour the Son even as they honour the Father. He who does not honour the Son does not honour the Father who sent him.

In truth, in truth, I say to you, he who hears my word, and believes him who sent me, has eternal life, and does not come into judgment, but has passed out of death into life.

In truth, in truth, I say to you: an hour is coming and now is, when the dead will hear the voice of the Son of God, and those who hear will live. For just as the Father has life in himself, even so he gave to the Son also to have life in himself; and he gave him authority to execute judgment, because he is the Son of Man. Do not be astonished by this; for an hour is coming, in which all who are in the tombs will hear his voice, and will come forth; those who did the good deeds to a resurrection of life, those who committed the evil deeds to a resurrection of judgment.

I can do nothing on my own initiative. As I hear, I judge; and my judgment is just, because I do not seek my own will, but the will of him who sent me.

If I alone testify about myself, my testimony is not (true), but there is (someone) who testifies of me, and I know that the testimony which he gives about me is true. You have sent to John, and he has testified to the truth. But the testimony which I receive is not from man, but I say these things so that you may be saved. It was he who was the lamp that burned and shone. You were willing to rejoice for a while in his light.

But the testimony which I have is greater than the testimony of John; for the works which the Father has given me to accomplish, the very works that I do, testify about me, that the Father has sent me.

And the Father who sent me, He has testified of me. You have neither heard his voice at any time nor seen his face. You do not have his word abiding in you, for you do not believe him whom he sent.

You examine the Scriptures because you think that in them you have eternal life; it is these that testify about me; and you are unwilling to come to me so that you may have life. I do not receive glory from men; but I know you, that you do not have the love of God in yourselves. I have come in my Father's name, and you do not receive me; if another comes in his own name, you will receive him. How can you believe, when you receive glory from one another and you do not seek the glory that is from the one and only God? Do not think that I will accuse you before the Father; the one who accuses you is Moses, in whom you have set your hope. For if you believed Moses; you would believe me, for he wrote about me. But if you do not believe his writings, how will you believe my words?

SIXTH GOSPEL

Jesus himself went away beyond the Sea of Galilee (or Tiberias). A large crowd followed him, because they saw the signs which he was performing on those who were sick. Then Jesus went up on the mountain, and there he sat down with his Disciples. Now Passover was near, it was the feast of the Jews. Jesus seeing that a large crowd was coming to him, said to Philip: Where are we to buy bread, so that these may eat? One of his Disciples, Andrew, Simon Peter's brother, said to him: There is a man here who has some barley loaves and fish, but what are these for so many people? Jesus then took the loaves, and having given thanks, he distributed to those who were seated; likewise also of the fish as much as they wanted. When they were filled, he said to his Disciples: Gather up the crumbs that are left so that nothing will be lost. So they gathered them up, and distributed them to the poor, and they admired the love of Jesus for them, and they said amongst themselves: If he was our master, we would always eat. Jesus, therefore, knowing that they were coming to make him king, withdrew himself again, alone, to the mountain.

But the evening came, and his Disciples went down to the sea, and after getting into a boat, they started to cross the sea to Capernaum. It had already become dark, and Jesus had not yet come to them. A great wind blew and the sea began to be stirred up. Then, when they had rowed about twenty-five or thirty *stadia*[5] , they saw Jesus coming on the sea and drawing near to the boat; and the storm became stronger. But he said to them: Do not be afraid. So they were willing to receive him into the boat, and then the boat was at the land. The next day those whom Jesus had fed and those who had seen him on the sea got in their boats and went to find Jesus at Capernaum. And he told them: In truth, in truth I say to you, you seek me, not because you saw signs, but because you ate of the loaves and were filled. Do not work for the food which perishes, but for the food which endures to eternal life, which the Son of Man will give to you, for on him the Father, God, has set his seal. Therefore they said to him: What shall we do, so that we may work the works of God? Jesus answered and said to them: This is the work of God, that you believe in him whom he has sent. So they said to him: What then do you do for a sign, so that we may see, and believe you? What work do you perform? Our fathers ate the manna in the wilderness; as it is written, 'He gave them bread out of heaven to eat'. Jesus then said to them: In truth, in truth, I say to you, it is not Moses who has given you the bread out of heaven, but it is my Father who gives you the true bread (from above) out of heaven. For the bread of God is that which comes down out of heaven, and gives life to the world. Then they said to him: Lord, always give us this bread.

Jesus said to them: I am the bread of life; he who comes to me will not hunger, and he who believes in me will never thirst. But I said to you that you have seen me, and yet do not believe. All that the Father gives me will come to me, and the one who comes to me I will certainly not cast out. For I have come down from heaven, not to do my own will, but the will of him who sent me. This is the will of him who sent me, that of all that he has given me I lose nothing, but raise it up on the last day. For this is the will of the one who sent me, that all (mankind) who beholds the Son and believes in him will have eternal life.

Therefore the Jews were grumbling about him, because he said: I am the bread that came down out of heaven. They were saying: Is not this Jesus, the son of Joseph, whose father and mother we know? How does he now say, 'I have come down out of heaven'? Is it because he lived with the Greeks that he has come thus to converse with us? What is there in common with what he learned from the Egyptians, and that which our fathers taught us? Jesus answered and said to them: Do not grumble among yourselves. No one can come to me unless the Father who sent me draws him; and I will raise him up on the last day. It is written in the prophets: And they shall all be taught of God. Everyone who has heard and learned from the Father, comes to me. Not that anyone has seen the Father, except the one who is from God; he has seen the Father. In truth, in truth, I say to you, he who believes has eternal life. I am the bread of life. Our fathers ate the manna in the wilderness, and they died. This is the bread and the wine which came down from Heaven, so that one may eat of it and not die. I am the living bread that came down out of heaven; if anyone eats and drinks of these, he will live forever; I am the living bread which has come down from Heaven. If someone eats it and drinks it, they will live forever.

Then the Jews began to argue with one another, saying: How can this man give us His flesh to eat? So Jesus said to them: In truth, in truth, I say to you, unless you eat the flesh of the Son of man and drink his blood, you have no life in yourselves. He

42

who eats my flesh and drinks my blood has eternal life, and I will raise him up on the last day. For my flesh is true food, and my blood is true drink. He who eats my flesh and drinks my blood abides in me, and I in him. As the living Father sent me, and I live because of the Father, so he who eats me, he also will live because of me. This is the bread which came down out of Heaven; not as the fathers ate and died; he who eats this bread will live forever.

These things he said in the synagogue as he taught in Capernaum. Therefore many of his Disciples, when they heard this said: his is a difficult statement; who can listen to it? But Jesus, conscious that his disciples grumbled at this, said to them: Does this cause you to stumble? It is the Spirit who gives life; the flesh profits nothing; the words that I have spoken to you are spirit and are life. But there are some of you who do not believe. And he said: For this reason I have said to you, that no one can come to me unless it has been granted him from my Father.

From that (moment) many of his Disciples withdrew and were not walking with him anymore. So Jesus said to the twelve: You do not want to go away also, do you? Simon Peter answered him: Lord, to whom shall we go? You have words of eternal life. We have believed and have come to know that you are the Christ, the living Son of God. Jesus answered them: Did I myself not choose you, the twelve, as well as it was prescribed to me, when I received the strength from above, to teach in the Father and the Holy Spirit, and that I give you with the spirit, the power that I received from the Father and Spirit, in the temple where the bread of life eternal is kept.

SEVENTH GOSPEL

And Jesus after this lived in Galilee. He was unwilling to live in Judea because the Jews were seeking to kill him. Now the feast of the Jews, the Feast of Tabernacles[6], was near. Therefore his brothers said to him: Leave here and go into Judea, so that your disciples also may see your works which You are doing. For no one does anything in secret when he himself seeks to be known publicly. If you do these things, show yourself to the world. For not even his brothers were believing in him. So Jesus said to them: My time is not yet here, but your time is always opportune. The world cannot hate you, but it hates me because I testify of it, that its deeds are evil. Go up to the feast yourselves; I do not go up to this feast because my time has not yet fully come. Having said these things to them, he stayed in Galilee.

But when His brothers had gone up to the feast, then he Himself also went up, not publicly, but as if, in secret. So the Jews were seeking him at the feast and were saying: Where is he? And there was much grumbling among the crowds concerning him; some were saying: He is a good man; others were saying: No, on the contrary, he leads the people astray. Yet no one was speaking openly of him for fear of the Jews. But when it was now the midst of the feast Jesus went up into the Temple, and began to teach. The Jews then were astonished, saying: How has this man learned letters, never having learned them, except Greek letters? So Jesus answered them and said: My teaching[7] is not mine, but his who sent me. If anyone is willing to do his will, he will know of the teaching, whether it is of God or whether I speak from myself. He who speaks from himself seeks his own glory; but he who is seeking the glory of the one who sent him, he is true, and there is no unrighteousness in him.

Did not Moses give you the Law, and yet none of you carries out the Law? And none of you lives it. I come therefore in order to convert you to the law. The crowd answered: You have a demon! Who seeks to kill you? Jesus answered them: I did one deed, and you are all astonished. For this reason Moses has given you circumcision, not because it is from Moses, but from our fathers, and on the Sabbath you circumcise a man. If a man receives circumcision on the Sabbath so that the Law of Moses will not be broken, are you angry with me because I made an entire man well on the Sabbath? Do not judge according to appearance, but be just.

So some of the people of Jerusalem were saying: Is this not the man whom they are seeking to kill? Look, he is speaking publicly, and they are saying nothing to him. The magistrates do not really know that this is the Christ, do they? However, we know where this man is from; but whenever the Christ may come, no one knows where he is from. Then Jesus cried out in the Temple, teaching and saying: You both know me and know where I am from; and I have not come of myself, but he who sent me is true, whom you do not know. I know him, because I am from him, and he sent me. So they were seeking to seize him; and no man laid his hand on him, because his hour had not yet come. But many of the crowd believed in him; and they were saying: When the Christ comes, he will not perform more signs than those which this man has, will he?

The Pharisees heard the crowd muttering these things about him, and the chief priests and the Pharisees sent officers to seize him. Therefore Jesus said: For a little while longer I am with you, then I go to him who sent me. You will seek me, and will not find me; and where I am, you cannot come. The Jews then said to one another: Where does this man intend to go that we will not find him? He is not intending to go to the Dispersion among the Greeks, and teach the Greeks, is he? What is this statement that he said: 'You will seek me, and will not find me; and where I am, you cannot come'? Now on the last day, the great day of the feast, Jesus stood and cried out, saying, "If anyone is thirsty, let him come to me and drink. He who believes in me, as the Scripture said, 'From his body will flow rivers of living water.' But this he spoke of the Spirit, whom those who believed in him were to receive; for the Spirit was not yet given, because Jesus was not yet glorified.

Some of the people therefore, when they heard these words, were saying: This certainly is the Prophet. Others were saying: This is the Christ. Still others were saying: Surely the Christ is not going to come from Galilee, is he? Has not the Scripture said that the Christ comes from the spirit (the descendants) of David, and from Bethlehem, the village where David was born? So a division occurred in the crowd because of him. Some of them wanted to seize him, but no one laid hands on him.

The officers then came to the chief priests and Pharisees, and they said to them: Why did you not bring him? The officers answered: Never has a man spoken the way this man speaks. The Pharisees then answered them: You have not also been led astray, have you? No one of the rulers or Pharisees has believed in him, has he? But this crowd which does not know the Law is accursed. Nicodemus (he who came to Him before, being one of them) said to them: Our Law does not judge a man unless it first hears from him and knows what he is doing, does it? They answered him: You are not also from Galilee, are you? Search, and see that no prophet arises out of Galilee. Everyone went to his home, but Jesus went to the Mount of Olives.

✳ EIGHTH GOSPEL

Early in the morning, Jesus came again into the Temple, and all the people were coming to him; and he sat down and began to teach them. The scribes and the Pharisees brought a woman caught in adultery, and having set her in the centre of the Court, they said to him: Teacher, this woman has been caught in adultery, in the very act. Now in the Law Moses commanded us to stone such women; what then do you say? They were saying this, testing him, so that they might have grounds for accusing him. But Jesus stooped down and with his finger wrote on the ground. But when they persisted in asking him, he straightened up, and said to them: He who is without sin among you, let him be the first to throw a stone at her. Again he stooped down and wrote on the ground. When they heard it, they began to go out one by one, beginning with the older ones, and he was left alone, and the woman, where she was, in the centre of the Court. Straightening up, Jesus said to her: Woman, where are they? Did no one condemn you? She said: No one, Lord. And Jesus said: I do not condemn you, either. Go. From now on sin no more.

Then Jesus again spoke to them, saying: I am the Light of the world; he who follows me will not walk in the darkness, but will have the Light of life. So the Pharisees said to him: You are testifying about yourself; your testimony is not true. Jesus answered and said to them: Even if I testify about myself, my testimony is true, for I know where I came from and where I am going; but you do not know where I come from or where I am going. You judge according to the flesh; I am not judging anyone. But even if I do judge, my judgment is true; for I am not alone in it, but I and the Father who sent me. Even in your law it has been written that the testimony of two men is true. I am he who testifies about myself, and the Father who sent me testifies about me. So they were saying to him: Where is your Father? Jesus answered: You know neither me nor my Father; if you knew me, you would know My Father also. These words he spoke in the treasury, as he taught in the Temple; and no one seized him, because his hour had not yet come. Then he said again to them: I go away, and you will seek me, and will die in your sin; where I am going, you cannot come. So the Jews were saying: Surely he will not kill himself, will He, since he says: Where I am going, you cannot come? And He was saying to them: You are from below, I am from above; you are of this world, I am not of this world. Therefore I said to you that you will die in your sins; for unless you believe that I am he, you will die in your sins. So they were saying to him: Who are you? Jesus said to them: What have

I been saying to you from the beginning? I have many things to speak and to judge concerning you, but he who sent me is true; and the things which I heard from him, these I speak to the world. They did not realize that he had been speaking to them about the Father. So Jesus said: When you lift up the Son of man, then you will know that I am he, and I do nothing on my own initiative, but I speak these things as the Father taught me. And he who sent me is with me; he has not left me alone, for I always do the things that are pleasing to him. As he spoke these things, many came to believe in him.

So Jesus was saying to those Jews who had believed him: If you continue in my word, then you are truly disciples of mine; and you will know the truth, and the truth will make you free. They answered him: We are Abraham's descendants and have never yet been enslaved to anyone; how is it that you say: 'You will become free'?

Jesus answered them: In truth, in truth, I say to you, everyone who commits sin is the slave of sin. The slave does not remain in the house forever; the son does remain forever. So if the Son makes you free, you will be free indeed. I know that you are Abraham's descendants; yet you seek to kill me, because my word has no place in you. I speak the things which I have seen with my Father; therefore you also do the things which you heard from your father.

They answered and said to him: Abraham is our father. Jesus said to them: If you are Abraham's children, do the deeds of Abraham. But as it is, you are seeking to kill me, a man who has told you the truth, which I heard from God; this Abraham did not do. You are doing the deeds of your father. They said to him: We were not born of fornication; we have one Father: God. Jesus said to them: If God were your Father, you would love me, for I proceeded forth and have come from God, for I have not even come on my own initiative, but he sent me. Why do you not understand what I am saying? It is because you cannot hear my word. You are of your father the devil, and you want to do the desires of your father. He was a murderer from the beginning, and does not stand in the truth because there is no truth in him. Whenever he speaks a lie, he speaks from his own nature, for he is a liar and the father of lies. But because I speak the truth, you do not believe me. Which one of you convicts me of sin? If I speak truth, why do you not believe me? He who is of God hears the words of God; for this reason you do not hear them, because you are not of God.

The Jews answered and said to him: Do we not say rightly that you are possessed by a demon? Jesus answered: I do not have a demon; but I honour my Father, and you dishonour me. But I do not seek my glory; there is one who seeks and judges. In truth, in truth, I say to you, if anyone keeps my word he will never see death. The Jews said to him: Now we know that you have a demon. Abraham died, and the prophets also; and you say: If anyone keeps my word, he will never taste of death. Surely you are not greater than our father Abraham, who died? The prophets died too; whom do you make yourself out to be? Jesus answered: If I glorify myself, my glory is nothing; it is my Father who glorifies me, of whom you say: He is our God, and you have not come to know him, but I know him; and if I say that I do not know him, I will be a liar like you, but I do know him and keep his word. Your father Abraham rejoiced to see my day, and he saw it and was glad. So the Jews said to him: You are not yet fifty years old, and have you seen Abraham? Jesus said to them: In truth, in truth, I say to you, before Abraham was born, I am. Therefore they picked up stones to throw at him, but Jesus hid himself and went out of the Temple.

✳

NINTH GOSPEL

As Jesus passed by, he saw a man blind from birth. And his Disciples asked him: Rabbi, who sinned, this man or his parents, that he would be born blind? Jesus answered: It was neither that this man sinned, nor his parents; but it was so that the works of God might be displayed in him. We must work the works of him who sent me as long as it is day; night is coming when no one can work. While I am in the world, I am the Light of the world. When he had said this, he spat on the ground, and made clay of the spittle, and applied the clay to his eyes, and said to him: Go, wash in the pool of Siloam. So he went away and washed, and came back seeing. Therefore the neighbours, and those who previously saw him as a beggar, were saying: Is not this the one who used to sit and beg? Others were saying: This is he; still others were saying: No, but he is like him. He kept saying: I am the one. So they were saying to him: How then were your eyes opened? He answered: The man who is called Jesus made clay, and anointed my eyes, and said to me: Go to Siloam and wash; so I went away and washed, and I received sight. They said to him: Where is he? He said: I do not know. They brought the man who had been blind to the Pharisees. Now it was a Sabbath on

51

the day when Jesus made the clay and opened his eyes. Then the Pharisees also were asking him again how he received his sight. And he said to them: He applied clay to my eyes, and I washed, and I see. Therefore some of the Pharisees were saying: This man is not from God, because he does not keep the Sabbath. But others were saying: How can a man who is a sinner perform such signs? And there was a division among them. So they said to the blind man again: What do you say about him, since he opened your eyes? And he said: He is a Prophet.

The Jews then did not believe it of him, that he had been blind and had received sight, until they called the parents of the very one who had received his sight, and questioned them, saying: Is this your son, who you say was born blind? Then how does he now see? His parents answered them and said: We know that this is our son, and that he was born blind; but how he now sees, we do not know; or who opened his eyes, we do not know. Ask him; he is of age, he will speak for himself. His parents said this because they were afraid of the Jews; for the Jews had already agreed that if anyone confessed him to be the Christ, he was to be put out of the Synagogue. For this reason his parents said: He is of age; ask him.

So a second time they called the man who had been blind, and said to him: Give glory to God; we know that this man is a sinner. He then answered: Whether he is a sinner, I do not know; one thing I do know, that though I was blind, now I see. So they said to him: What did he do to you? How did he open your eyes? He answered them: I told you already and you did not listen; why do you want to hear it again? You do not want to become his disciples too, do you? They reviled him and said: You are his disciple, but we are disciples of Moses. We know that God has spoken to Moses, but as for this man, we do not know where he is from. The man answered and said to them: Well, here is an amazing thing, that you do not know where he is from, and yet he opened my eyes. We know that God does not hear sinners; but if anyone is God-fearing and does his will, he hears him. Since the beginning of time it has never been heard that anyone opened the eyes of a person born blind. If this man were not from God, he could do nothing. They answered him: You were born entirely in sins, and are you teaching us? So they put him out. Jesus heard that they had put him out, and finding him, he said: Do you believe in the Son of God? He answered: Who is he, Lord, that I may believe in him? Jesus said to him: You have both seen him, and he is the one who is talking with you. And he said: Lord, I believe. And he prostrated himself before him. And Jesus said: For judgment I came into this world, so that those who do not see may see, and that those who see may become blind. Those of the Pharisees who were with him heard these things and said to him: We are not blind too, are we? Jesus said to them: If you were blind, you would have no sin; but since you say: 'We see,' your sin remains.

✳
TENTH GOSPEL

Jesus having again met the Pharisees was asked (by them): How is it that you come from God? Jesus responded: In truth, in truth, I say to you, he who does not enter by the door into the fold of the sheep, but climbs up some other way, he is a thief and a robber. But he who enters by the door is a shepherd of the sheep. To him the doorkeeper opens, and the sheep hear his voice, and he calls his own sheep by name and leads them out. When he puts forth all his own, he goes ahead of them, and the sheep follow him because they know his voice. A stranger they simply will not follow, but will flee from him, because they do not know the voice of strangers. This figure of speech Jesus spoke to them, but they did not understand what those things were which he had been saying to them.

Jesus said to them again: In truth, in truth, I say to you, I am the door of the sheep. All who came before me are thieves and robbers, but the sheep did not hear them. I am the door; if anyone enters through me, he will be saved, and will go in and out and find pasture. The thief comes only to steal and kill and destroy; I came that they may have life, and have it abundantly. I am the good shepherd; the good shepherd lays down his life for the sheep. He who is a hired hand, and not a shepherd, who is not the owner of the sheep, sees the wolf coming, and leaves the sheep and flees, and the wolf snatches them and scatters them. He flees because he is a hired hand and is not concerned about the sheep. I am the good shepherd, and I know my own and my own know me, even as the Father knows me and I know the Father; and I lay down my life for the sheep. I have other sheep, which are not of this fold; I must bring them also, and they will hear my voice; and they will become one flock with one shepherd. For this reason the Father loves me, because I lay down my life so that I may take it again. No one has taken it away from me, but I lay it down on my own initiative. I have authority to lay it down, and I have authority to take it up again. This commandment I received from my Father.

A division occurred again among the Jews because of these words. Many of them were saying: He has a demon and is insane. Why do you listen to Him? Others were saying: These are not the sayings of one demon-possessed. A demon cannot open the eyes of the blind, can he?

At that time the Feast of the Dedication took place at Jerusalem, and it was winter, and Jesus was walking in the Temple in the portico of Solomon. The Jews then gathered around him, and were saying to him: How long will you keep us in suspense? If you are the Christ, tell us plainly. Jesus answered them: I told you, and you do not believe; the works that I do in my Father's name, these testify of me. But you do not believe because you are not of my sheep. My sheep hear my voice, and I know them, and they follow me; and I give eternal life to them, and they will never perish; and no one will snatch them out of my hand. My Father, who has given them to me, is greater than all; and no one is able to snatch them out of the Father's hand. I and the Father are one.

The Jews picked up stones again to stone him. Jesus answered them: I showed you many good works from the Father; for which of them are you stoning me? The Jews answered him: For a good work we do not stone you, but for blasphemy; and because you, being a man, make yourself out to be God. Jesus answered them: Has it not been written in your Law, I said, you are gods? If he called them gods, to whom the word of God came (and the Scripture cannot be broken), do you say of him, whom the Father sanctified and sent into the world: 'You are blaspheming,' because I said, 'I am the Son of God'? If I do not do the works of my Father, do not believe me; but if I do them, though you do not believe me, believe the works, so that you may know and understand that the Father is in me, and I in the Father. Therefore they were seeking again to seize him, and he eluded their grasp. And he went away again beyond the Jordan to the place where John was first baptizing, and he was staying there. Many came to him and were saying: While John performed no sign, yet everything John said about this man was true. Many believed in him there.

✳
ELEVENTH GOSPEL

Nevertheless there was a man of Bethany, Lazarus, who was sick, from the village of Mary and her sister Martha. It was the Mary who anointed the Lord with myrrh, and wiped his feet with her hair, whose brother Lazarus was sick. So the sisters sent word to him, saying: Lord, behold, he whom you love is sick. But when Jesus heard this, he said: This sickness is not to end in death, but for the glory of God, so that the Son of God may be glorified by it. Now Jesus loved Martha and her sister and Lazarus. So when he heard that he was sick, he then stayed two days longer in the place where he was. Then after this he said to the Disciples: Let us go to Judea again. The Disciples said to him: Master[8] , the Jews were just now seeking to stone you, and are you going there again? Jesus answered: Are there not twelve hours in the day? If anyone walks in the day, he does not stumble, because he sees the light of this world. But if anyone walks in the night, he stumbles, because the light is not in him. This he said, and after that he said to them: Our friend Lazarus has fallen asleep; but I go, so that I may awaken him. The Disciples then said to him: Lord, if he has fallen asleep, he will recover. Now Jesus had spoken of his death, but they thought that He was speaking of literal sleep. So when Jesus came, he found that he had already been in the tomb four days. Now Bethany was near Jerusalem, about fifteen stadia (two miles) off; and many of the Jews had come to Martha and Mary, to console them concerning their brother. Martha therefore, when she heard that Jesus was coming, went to meet him, but Mary stayed at the house. Martha then said to Jesus: Lord, if you had been here, my brother would not have died. Even now I know that whatever you ask of God, God will give you. Jesus said to her: Your brother is asleep. And everyone answered him: No he is dead. Jesus said to them: If he is truly dead, he will in any case be resurrected. Martha said to him: I know that he will rise again in the resurrection on the last day. Jesus said to her: I am the resurrection and the life; he who believes in me will live even if he dies, and everyone who lives and believes in me will never die. Do you believe this? She said to him: Yes, Lord; I have believed that you are the Christ, the Son of God, even he who comes into the world. When she had said this, she went away and called Mary her sister, saying secretly: The Master is here and is calling for you. And when she heard it, she got up quickly and was coming to him.

Now Jesus had not yet come into the village, but was still in the place where Martha met him. Then the Jews who were with her in the house, and consoling her, when they saw that Mary got up quickly and went out, they followed her, supposing that she was going to the tomb to weep there. Therefore, when Mary came where Jesus was, she saw him, and fell at his feet, saying to him: Lord, if you had been here, my brother would not have died. When Jesus therefore saw her weeping, and the Jews who came with her also weeping, He was deeply moved in spirit and was troubled, and said: Where have you laid him? They said to him: Lord, come and see. Jesus wept. So the Jews were saying: See how he loved him! But some of them said: Could not this man, who opened the eyes of the blind man, have kept this man also from dying?

So Jesus, again being deeply moved within, came to the tomb. Now it was a cave, and a stone was lying against it. Jesus said: Remove the stone. Martha, the sister of the deceased, said to him: Lord, by this time there will be a stench, for he has been dead four days. Jesus said to her: Did I not say to you that if you believe, you will see the glory of God? So they removed the stone. Then Jesus raised his eyes, and said: Father, I thank you that you have heard me. I knew that you always hear me; but because of the people standing around I said it, so that they may believe that you sent me. When he had said these things, he cried out with a loud voice: Lazarus, come forth. The man who had died came forth, bound hand and foot with wrappings, and his face was wrapped around with a cloth. Jesus said to them: Unbind him, and let him go.

59

Therefore many of the Jews who came to Mary, and saw what he had done, believed in him. But some of them went to the Pharisees and told them the things which Jesus had done.

Therefore the chief priests and the Pharisees convened a council, and were saying: What are we doing? For this man is performing many signs. If we let Him go on like this, all men will believe in him, and the Romans will come and take away both our place and our nation. But one of them, Caiaphas, who was high priest that year, said to them: You know nothing at all, nor do you take into account that it is expedient for you that one man die for the people, and that the whole nation not perish. Now he did not say this on his own initiative, but being high priest that year, he prophesied that Jesus was going to die for the nation, and not for the nation only, but in order that he might also gather together into one the children of God who are scattered abroad. So from that day on they planned together to kill him.

Therefore Jesus no longer continued to walk publicly among the Jews, but went away from there to the country near the wilderness, into a city called Ephraim; and there he stayed with the disciples.

Now the Passover of the Jews was near, and many went up to Jerusalem out of the country before the Passover to purify themselves. So they were seeking for Jesus, and were saying to one another as they stood in the Temple: What do you think; that he will not come to the feast at all? Now the chief priests and the Pharisees had given orders that if anyone knew where He was, he was to report it, so that they might seize him.

✴
TWELFTH GOSPEL

Jesus, therefore, six days before the Passover, came to Bethany where he made Lazarus leave the tomb. So they made him a supper there, and Martha was serving. Lazarus was one of the guests. Mary then took a pound of very costly perfume of pure nard, and anointed the feet of Jesus and wiped his feet with her hair. The house was filled with the fragrance of the perfume. One of his Disciples, Judas Iscariot, (son of) Simon who was intending to betray him, said: Why was this perfume not sold for three hundred denarii and given to poor people? Now he said this, not because he was concerned about the poor, but because he was a thief, and as he had the money box, he used to pilfer what was put into it. Therefore Jesus said: Let her alone, so that she may keep it for the day of my burial. For you always have the poor with you, but you do not always have me.

The large crowd of the Jews then learned that he was there; and they came, not for Jesus' sake only, but that they might also see Lazarus. But the chief priests planned to put Lazarus to death also; because on account of him many of the Jews were going away and were believing in Jesus.

On the next day the large crowd who had come to the feast, when they heard that Jesus was coming to Jerusalem, took the branches of the palm trees and went out to meet Him, and began to shout: Hosanna! Blessed be him who comes in the name of the Lord, the King of Israel. So the people, who were with him when he called Lazarus out of the tomb continued to testify about him. For this reason also the people went and met Him, because they heard that He had performed this sign. So the Pharisees said to one another: You see that you are not doing any good; look, the world has gone after him.

Now there were some Greeks among those who were going up to worship at the feast; these then came to Philip, who was from Bethsaida of Galilee, and began to ask him, saying: Sir, we wish to see Jesus. Philip came and told Andrew; Andrew and Philip came and told Jesus. And Jesus answered them, saying: The hour has come for the Son of man to be glorified. In truth, in truth, I say to you, unless a grain of wheat falls into the earth and dies, it remains alone; but if it dies, it bears much fruit. He who loves his life loses it, and he who hates his life in this world will keep it to life eternal. If anyone serves me, he must follow me; and where I am, there my servant will be also; if anyone serves me, the Father will honour him.

Now my soul has become troubled; and what shall I say, 'Father, save me from this hour'? But for this purpose I came to this hour. Father, glorify Your name. Then a voice came out of heaven: I have both glorified it, and will glorify it again. So the crowd of people who stood by and heard it were saying that it had thundered; others were saying: An angel has spoken to him. Jesus answered and said: This voice has not come for my sake, but for your sakes. Now judgment is upon this world; now the ruler of this world will be cast out. And I, if I am lifted up from the earth, will draw all men to myself. The crowd then answered him: We have heard out of the Law that the Christ is to remain forever; and how can you say, 'The Son of man must be lifted up'?

Who is this Son of man? So Jesus said to them: For a little while longer the Light is among you. Walk while you have the Light, so that darkness will not overtake you; he who walks in the darkness does not know where he goes. While you have the Light, believe in the Light, so that you may become sons of Light.

These things Jesus spoke, and he went away and hid himself from them. But though he had performed so many signs before them, yet they were not believing in him. This was to fulfill the word of Isaiah the prophet which he spoke: Lord, who has believed our report? And to whom has the arm of the Lord been revealed? For this reason they could not believe, for Isaiah said again: He has blinded their eyes and hardened their heart, so that they would not see with their eyes and perceive with their heart, and be converted and I heal them. These things Isaiah said because he saw His glory, and he spoke of Him. Nevertheless many even of the rulers believed in him, but because of the Pharisees they were not confessing him, for fear that they would be put out of the Synagogue; for they loved the approval of men rather than the approval of God.

And Jesus cried out and said: He who believes in me, does not believe in me but in Him who sent me. He who sees me sees the One who sent me. I have come as Light into the world, so that everyone who believes in me will not remain in darkness. If anyone hears my sayings and does not keep them, I do not judge him; for I did not come to judge the world, but to save it. He who rejects me and does not receive my sayings, has (someone) who judges him; that being the word which I have spoken to him. It (the word) will judge him in the last day. For

I did not speak for myself, but the Father Himself who sent me has given me a commandment as to what to say and what to speak. I know that His commandment is eternal life; therefore the things I speak, I speak just as the Father has told me.

✳ THIRTEENTH GOSPEL

Now before the Feast of the Passover, Jesus knowing that his hour had come that he would depart out of this world to the Father, having loved his own who were in the world, he loved them to the end. During supper, the Devil having already put into the heart of Judas Iscariot, (son) of Simon, to betray him, Jesus, knowing that the Father had given all things into his hands, and that he had come forth from God and was going back to God, got up from supper, and laid aside his garments; and taking a towel, he girded himself. Then he poured water into the basin, and began to wash the Disciples' feet and to wipe them with the towel with which he was girded. So when he had washed their feet, and taken his garments and reclined at the table again, He said to them: Do you know what I have done to you. You call me Master and Lord; and you are right, for so I am. If I then, the Lord and Master, washed your feet, you also ought to wash one another's feet, for I gave you an example that you also should do as I did to you. In truth, in truth, I say to you, a slave is not greater than his master, nor is one who is sent greater than the one who sent him. If you know these things, you are blessed if you do them. From now on I am telling you before it comes to pass, so that when it does occur, you may believe that I am he, in truth, in truth I say to you that one among you will betray me. And they looked at one another, uncertain of what he spoke. Then, one of the Disciples, the one whom Jesus loved, was reclining on Jesus' bosom. So Simon Peter gestured to him, and said to him:

Tell us who it is of whom he is speaking. He, leaning back thus on Jesus' bosom, said to him: Lord, who is it? Jesus then answered: That is the one for whom I shall dip the morsel and give it to him. So when he had dipped the morsel, he took and gave it to Judas Iscariot, (son) of Simon. Therefore Jesus said to him: What you do, do quickly. Now no one of those reclining at the table knew for what purpose he had said this to him. For some were supposing, because Judas had the money box, that Jesus was saying to him, "Buy the things we have need of for the feast"; or else, that he should give something to the poor. So after receiving the morsel he went out immediately; and it was night.

FOURTEENTH GOSPEL

Therefore when he had gone out, Jesus said: Now is the Son of man glorified, and God is glorified in him; if God is glorified in him, God will also glorify him in Himself, and will glorify him immediately. Little children, I am with you a little (while) longer. You will seek me; and as I said to the Jews, now I also say to you, 'Where I am going, you cannot come.' A new commandment I give to you, that you love one another, even as I have loved you, that you also love one another. By this all men will know that you are my Disciples, if you have love (charity) for one another. Judas returned where Jesus was and but Jesus continued and said: You believe in God so that your heart is not troubled, and you believe in me. In my Father's house are many dwelling places; if it were not so, I would have told you; for I go to prepare a place for you. If I go and prepare a place for you, I will come again and receive you to myself, that where I am, there you may be also. And you know the way where I am going. Thomas said to him: Lord, we do not know where you are going, how do we know the way? Jesus said to him: I am the way, and the truth, and the life; no one comes to the Father but through me. If you had known me, you would have known my Father also; from now on you know Him, and have seen Him. Philip said to him: Lord, show us the Father, and it is enough for us. Jesus said to him: Have I been so long with you, and yet you have not come to know me, Philip? He who has seen me has seen the Father; how can you say, 'Show us the Father'? Do you not believe that I am in the Father, and the Father is in me?

The words that I say to you I do not speak on my own initiative, but the Father abiding in me does His works. Believe me that I am in the Father and the Father is in me; otherwise believe because of the works themselves. In truth, in truth, I say to you, he who believes in me, the works that I do, he will do also; and greater works than these he will do; because I go to the Father. Whatever you ask in my name, that will I do, so that the Father may be glorified in the Son. If you ask me anything in my name, I will do it. If you love me, you will keep my commandments. I will ask the Father, and He will give you another comforter, that He may be with you forever. That is the Spirit of truth, whom the world cannot receive, because it does not see it or know it, but you know it because it abides with you and will be in you. I will not leave you as orphans; I will come to you. After a little while the world will no longer see me, but you will see me; because I live, you will live also. In that day you will know that I am in my Father, and you in me, and I in you. He who has my commandments and keeps them is the one who loves me; and he who loves me will be loved by my Father, and I will love him and will disclose myself to him. Judas (not Iscariot) said to him: Lord, what then has happened that you are going to disclose yourself to us and not to the world? Jesus answered and said to him: If anyone loves me, he will keep my word; and my Father will love him, and we will come to him and make our abode with him. He who does not love me does not keep my words; and the word which you hear is not mine, but the Father's who sent me. These things I have spoken to you while abiding with you. But the comforter, the Holy Spirit, whom the Father will send in my name, will teach you all things, and bring to your remembrance all that I said to you.

Peace I leave with you; my peace I give to you; not as the world gives do I give to you. Do not let your heart be troubled, nor let it be fearful. You heard that I said to you, 'I go away, and I will come to you.' If you loved me, you would have rejoiced because I go to the Father, for the Father is greater than I. Now I have told you before it happens, so that when it happens, you may believe. I will not speak much more with you, for the ruler of the world is coming, and he has nothing in me; but so that the world may know that I love the Father, I do exactly as the Father commanded me. Get up, let us go from here.

✳

FIFTEENTH GOSPEL

They continued to walk. And Jesus turned to his Disciples and said: You have understood what I told you: I am the true vine, and my Father is the vinedresser. Every branch in me that does not bear fruit, He takes away; and every branch that bears fruit, He prunes it so that it may bear more fruit. You are already clean because of the word which I have spoken to you. Abide in me, and I in you. As the branch cannot bear fruit of itself unless it abides in the vine, so neither can you unless you abide in me. I am the vine, you are the branches; he who abides in me and I in him, he bears much fruit, for apart from me you can do nothing. If anyone does not abide in me, he is thrown away as a branch and dries up; and they gather them, and cast them into the fire and they are burned. If you abide in me, and my words abide in you, ask whatever you wish, and it will be done for you. My Father is glorified by this, that you bear much fruit, and so prove to be my Disciples. Just as the Father has loved me, I have also loved you; abide in my love. If you keep my commandments, you will abide in my love; just as I have kept my Father's commandments and abide in His love. These things I have spoken to you so that my joy may be in you, and that your joy may be made full.

This is my commandment, that you love one another, just as I have loved you. Greater love has no one than this: that one lay down his life for his friends. You are my friends if you do what I command you. No longer do I call you slaves, for the slave does not know what his master is doing. I have called you friends, for all things that I have heard from my Father I have made known to you, and I will give you the Holy Spirit, which is my Spirit as it is the Spirit of my Father. You did not choose me but I chose you, and appointed you that you would go and bear fruit, and that your fruit would remain, so that whatever you ask of the Father in my name He may give to you. This I command you, that you love one another. If the world hates you, you know that it has hated me before it hated you. If you were of the world, the world would love its own; but because you are not of the world, but I chose you out of the world, because of this the world hates you. Remember the word that I said to you, 'A slave is not greater than his master.' If they persecuted me, they will also persecute you; if they kept my word, they will keep yours also. But all these things they will do to you for my name's sake, because they do not know the One who sent me. If I had not come and spoken to them, they would not have sin, but now they have no excuse for their sin. He who hates me hates my Father also. If I had not done among them the works which no one else did, they would not have sin; but now they have both seen and hated me and my Father as well. But they have done this to fulfill the word that is written in their law: They hated me without a reason. When the Paraclete (helper), the Spirit of truth comes, whom I will give to you from the Father, and who proceeds from the Father and the Son, He will testify about me, and you will testify also, because you have been with me from the beginning.

SIXTEENTH GOSPEL

But Jesus having come back to himself said: These things I have spoken to you so that you may not be shocked. They will chase you from the Synagogue, but an hour is coming for everyone who kills you to think that he is offering service to God. These things they will do because they have not known the Father or me. But these things I have spoken to you, so that when their hour comes, you may remember that I told you of them. These things I did not say to you at the beginning, because I was with you. But now I am going to Him who sent me; and none of you asks me: Where are you going? But because I have said these things to you, pain has filled your heart. But I tell you the truth, it is to your advantage that I go away; for if I do not go away, the Paraclete will not come to you; but if I go, I will send Him to you. And He, when He comes, will convict the world concerning sin and justice and judgment; concerning sin, because they do not believe in me; and concerning justice, because I go to the

Father and you no longer see me; and concerning judgment, because the Prince of this world has been judged. I have many more things to say to you, but you cannot bear them now. But when He, the Spirit of truth, comes, He will guide you into all the truth; for he will not speak on his own initiative, but whatever he hears, he will speak; and he will disclose to you what is to come. He will glorify me, for He will take of mine and will disclose it to you. All things that the Father has are mine; therefore I said that He takes of mine and will disclose it to you. A little while, and you will no longer see me; and again a little while, and you will see me." Some of his Disciples then said to one another: What is this thing he is telling us, 'A little while, and you will not see me; and again a little while, and you will see me'; and, 'because I go to the Father'? So they were saying: What is this that he says, 'A little while'? We do not know what he is talking about. Jesus knew that they wished to question him, and he said to them: Are you deliberating together about this, that I said, 'A little while, and you will not see me, and again a little while, and you will see me'? In truth, in truth, I say to you, that you will weep and lament, but the world will rejoice; you will grieve, but your grief will be turned into joy. Whenever a woman is in labour she has pain, because her hour has come; but when she gives birth to the child, she no longer remembers the anguish because of the joy that a child has been born into the world. Therefore you too have the truth and pain now; but I will see you again, and your heart will rejoice, and no one will take your joy away from you. In that day you will not question me about anything. In truth, in truth, I say to you, if you ask the Father for anything in my name, He will give it to you. Until now you have asked for nothing in my name; ask and you will receive, so that your joy may be made full. These things I have spoken to you in parables; but a time is coming when I will no longer speak to you in parables, but will tell you plainly of the Father. In that day you will ask in my name, and I do not say to you that I will request of the Father on your behalf; for the Father Himself loves you, because you have loved me and have believed that I came forth from the Father. I came forth from the Father and have come into the world; I am leaving the world again and going to the Father. His disciples said: Lo, now you are speaking plainly and are not using a figure of speech. Now we know that you know all things, and have no need for anyone to question you; by this we believe that you came from God. Jesus answered them: Do you now believe? Behold, a time is coming, and has already come, for you to be scattered, each to his own home, and to leave me alone; and yet I am not alone, because the Father is with me. These things I have spoken to you, so that in me you may have peace. In the world you have tribulation, but take courage; I have overcome the world.

SEVENTEENTH GOSPEL

Jesus said this, and lifting his eyes toward Heaven he said: Father, the hour has come; glorify your Son, that the Son may glorify you, even as you gave him power over all flesh, that to all whom you have given him, he may give an eternal life; but life itself consists of living in you and in your Son, and in the Spirit whom we know, and who knows us. I glorified you on the earth, having accomplished the work which you have given me to do. Now, Father, glorify me together with yourself, with the glory which I had with you before the world was. I have manifested your name to the men whom you gave me out of the world; they were yours and you gave them to me, and they have kept your word. Now they have come to know that everything you have given me is from you; for the words which you gave me I have given to them; and they received them and truly understood that I came forth from you, and they believed that you sent me. I ask on their behalf; I do not ask on behalf of the world, but of those whom you have given me; for they are yours; and all things that are mine are yours, and yours are mine; and I have been glorified in them. I am no longer in the world; and yet they themselves are in the world, and I come to you. Holy Father, keep them in your name, the name which you have given me that they may be one even as we are. While I was with them, I was keeping them in your name which you have given me; and I guarded them and not one of them perished but the Son of perdition. But now I come to you; and these things I speak in the world so that they may have my joy made full in themselves. I have given them your word; and the world has hated them, because they are not of the world, even as I am not of the world. I do not ask you to take them out of the world, but to keep them from the evil one. They are not of the world, even as I am not of the world. Sanctify them in the truth; your word is truth. As you sent me into the world, I also have sent them into the world. For their sakes I sanctify myself, that they themselves also may be sanctified in truth. I do not ask on behalf of these alone, but for those also who believe in me through their word; that they may all be one; even as you,

Father, are in me and I in you, that they also may be in us, so that the world may believe that you sent me. The glory which you have given me I have given to them, that they may be one, just as we are one; I in them and you in me, that they may be perfected in unity, so that the world may know that you sent me, and loved them, even as you have loved me. Father, I desire that they also, whom you have given me, be with me where I am, so that they may see my glory which you have given me, for you loved me before all. O just Father, although the world has not known you, yet I have known you; and these have known that you sent me; and I have made your name known to them, and will make it known, so that the love with which you loved me may be in them, and I in them. Likewise, Jesus, having raised up his hands said to his Disciples: Now that the hour has come to drink from the chalice that the Father has given to me, I say to you that I send you as I have been sent; obey my commandments, teach as I have taught you, so that the world will know. This is the reason why you receive the Holy Spirit, for those sins you will have remitted will be remitted, and for those which are kept, they will be kept. You have understood that which I have spoken unto you: I am not of this world. The Paraclete is in you; teach in the Paraclete. As my Father sent me, I likewise send you. In truth, I say unto you that I am not of this world, but John will be your father until he comes to be with me in Paradise, and he will anoint in the Holy Spirit.

✳
EIGHTEENTH GOSPEL

When Jesus had spoken these words, he went forth with his Disciples over the ravine of the Kidron, where there was a garden, in which he entered with his Disciples. Now Judas also, who was betraying him, knew the place, for Jesus had often met there with his Disciples. Judas then, having received the Roman cohort and officers from the chief priests and the Pharisees, came there with lanterns and torches and weapons. So Jesus, knowing all the things that were coming upon him, went forth and said to them, "Whom do you seek? They answered him: Jesus the Nazarene. He said to them: I am he. And Judas also, who was betraying him, was standing with them. So when he said to them: I am he, they drew back and fell to the ground. Therefore he again asked them: Whom do you seek? And they said: Jesus the Nazarene. Jesus answered: I told you that I am he; so if you seek me, let these go their way, to fulfill the word which he spoke: Of those whom you have given me I lost not one. Simon Peter then, having a sword, drew it and struck the high priest's slave, and cut off his right ear; and the slave's name was Malchus. So Jesus said to Peter: Put the sword into the sheath; the cup which the Father has given me, shall I not drink it? So the Roman cohort and the commander and the officers of the Jews, arrested Jesus and bound him, and led him to Annas first; for he was father-in-law of Caiaphas, who was high priest that year. Now Caiaphas was the one who had advised the Jews that it was expedient for one man to die on behalf of the people. Simon Peter was following Jesus, and so was another Disciple.

Now that Disciple was known to the high priest, and entered with Jesus into the court of the high priest, but Peter was standing at the door outside. So the other Disciple, who was known to the high priest, went out and spoke to the doorkeeper, and brought Peter in. Then the slave-girl who kept the door said to Peter: You are not also one of this man's disciples, are you? He said, "I am not." Now the slaves and the officers were standing there, having made a charcoal fire, for it was cold and they were warming themselves; and Peter was also with them, standing and warming himself.

The high priest then questioned Jesus about his Disciples, and about his teaching. Jesus answered him: I have spoken openly to the world; I always taught in the Synagogue and in the Temple, where all the Jews come together; and I spoke nothing in secret. Why do you question me? Question those who have heard what I spoke to them; they know what I said. When he had said this, one of the officers standing nearby struck Jesus, saying: Is that the way you answer the high priest? Jesus answered him: If I have spoken wrongly, testify of the wrong; but if rightly, why do you strike me? So Annas sent him bound to Caiaphas the high priest. Now Simon Peter was standing and warming himself. So they said to him: You are not also one of his disciples, are you? He denied it, and said: I am not. One of the slaves of the high priest said: Did I not see you in the garden with him? Peter then denied it again. Then they led Jesus from Caiaphas into the Praetorium, and it was early; and they themselves did not enter into the Praetorium so that they would not be defiled, but might eat the Passover. Therefore Pilate went out to them and said: What accusation do you bring against this man? They answered and said to him: If this man were not an evildoer, we would not have delivered him to you? So Pilate said to them: Take him yourselves, and judge him according to your law. The Jews said to him: We are not permitted to put anyone to death. Therefore Pilate entered again into the Praetorium, and summoned Jesus and said to him: Are you the king of the Jews? Jesus answered: Are you saying this on your own initiative, or did others tell you about me? Pilate answered: I am not a Jew, am I? Your own nation and the chief priests delivered you to me; what have you done? Jesus answered: My kingdom is not of this world. If my kingdom were of this world, then my servants would be fighting so that I would not be handed over to the Jews; but now my kingdom is not of here. Therefore Pilate said to him: So you are a king? Jesus answered: It is you who says that I am king. I have come for the truth, and for that I came into the world; to give testimony of the truth. Everyone who is of the truth hears my voice. Pilate said to him: What is truth? And when he had said this, he went out again to the Jews and said to them: I find no guilt in him. But you have a custom that I release someone for you at the Passover; do you wish then that I release for you the King of the Jews? So they cried out again, saying, "Not this Man, but Barabbas." Now Barabbas was a thief.

✳

NINETEENTH GOSPEL

Pilate, having understood what the Jews were demanding, and seized with fear, took Jesus and whipped him. And the soldiers twisted together a crown of thorns and put it on his head, and put a purple robe on him; and they began to come up to him and say: Hail, King of the Jews! and to give him slaps in the face. Pilate came out again and said to them: Behold, I am bringing him out to you so that you may know that I find no guilt in him. Jesus then came out, wearing the crown of thorns and the purple robe. Pilate said to them: Behold, the man. So when the chief priests and the officers saw him, they cried out saying: Crucify, (him) crucify! Pilate said to them: Take him yourselves and crucify him, for I find no guilt in him. The Jews answered him: We have a law, and by that law he ought to die because he made himself out to be the Son of God. Therefore when Pilate heard this statement, he was even more afraid; and he entered into the Praetorium again and said to Jesus: Where are you from? But Jesus gave him no answer. So Pilate said to him: You do not speak to me? Do you not know that I have authority to release you, and I have authority to crucify you? Jesus answered: You would have no power over me, unless it had been given you from above; for this reason he who delivered me to you has the greater sin. As a result of this Pilate made efforts to release him, but the Jews cried out saying: If you release this man, you are no friend of Caesar; everyone who makes himself out to be a king opposes Caesar. Therefore when Pilate heard these words, he brought Jesus out, and sat down on the judgment seat at a place called *Lithostrotos*[9], but in Hebrew, Gabbatha. Now it was the day of preparation for the Passover; it was about the sixth hour. And he said to the Jews: Behold, your King. So they cried out: Away with him, away with him, crucify him! Pilate said to them: Shall I crucify your King? The chief priests answered: We have no king but Caesar. So he then handed him over to them to be crucified. They took Jesus, therefore, and he went out, bearing his own cross, to the place called the Place of a Skull, which is called in Hebrew, Golgotha. There they crucified him, and with him two other men, one on either side; and Jesus in between. Pilate also wrote an inscription and put it on the cross. It was written: JESUS THE NAZARENE, THE KING OF THE JEWS." Therefore many of the Jews read this inscription, for the place where Jesus was crucified was near the city; and it was written in Hebrew, Latin and in Greek. So the chief priests of the Jews were saying to Pilate: Do not write: 'The King of the Jews'; but that he said, 'I am King of the Jews.' Pilate answered: What I have written, I have written. Then the soldiers, when they had crucified Jesus, took his outer garments and made four parts, a part to every soldier and also the tunic; now the tunic was seamless, woven in one piece. Therefore the soldiers did these things. But standing by the cross of Jesus were his mother, and his mother's sister, Mary the daughter of Cleophas, and Mary Magdalene. When Jesus then saw his mother, and the Disciple whom he loved standing nearby, he said to his mother: Do not weep for I return to my Father and an eternal life. Behold, your son; he will take my place. Then he said to the Disciple: Behold, your mother! Next, having lowered his head, he gave up his spirit. Then the Jews, because it was the day of preparation, so that the bodies would not remain on the cross on the Sabbath for that Sabbath was a high day, asked Pilate that their legs might be broken, and that they might be taken away. So the soldiers came, and broke the legs of the first man and of the other who was crucified with him; but coming to Jesus, when they saw that he was already dead, they did not break his legs. But one of the soldiers pierced his side with a spear, and immediately blood and water came out. After these things Joseph of Arimathea, being a Disciple of Jesus, but a secret one for fear of the Jews, asked (the permission of) Pilate that he might take away the body of Jesus; and Pilate agreed. So he came and took away his body. Nicodemus, who had first come to him by night, also came, bringing a mixture of myrrh and aloes, about a hundred pounds weight. So they took the body of Jesus and bound it in linen **81** wrappings with the spices, as is the burial custom of the Jews. Now in the place where he was crucified there was a garden, and in the garden a new tomb in which no one had yet been laid. Therefore because of the Jewish day of preparation, since the tomb was nearby, they laid Jesus there. John the Disciple that Jesus loved gives testimony to the truth of this scripture so that you believe it, and so that you will teach it. ✲

END OF THE GOSPELS ACCORDING TO
THE PRIMITIVE CHURCH

82

NOTES

[1]Great Britain. Record Commission. La Commission des Archives d'Angleterre (Record Commission) aux savans et antiquaires francais. Paris : A. Guyot et Scribe, Imprimeurs du roi, rue Neuve-des-Petits- Champs, no. 37, 1834. QB803 .S45 1817.

[2]ἄνωθεν - anōthen, is translated as "from above." The original French "d'en haut" also means "from above", or "from on high." See: Strong's reference 509, NAS Exhaustive Concordance of the Bible with Hebrew-Aramaic and Greek Dictionaries

[3]"Salut"in the original French. "Salut" in the religious context means "salvation."

[4]Piscine Probatique : Reservoir near the Temple of Solomon, in English translations this place is called "Sheep's Gate." "Probaton" in Greek, προβατον, προβατιον signifies small four-legged animals, i.e., goats and sheep. This pool was therefore most likely a watering hole for shepherds outside the walls of the city.

[5]Through Latin, stadium from the ancient Greek στάδιον stadion; a measure de 600 Greek feet or 625 Roman feet; approximately 180 metres. 3 stadia would therefore be 5.4km; between 3 and 4 miles.

[6]Literally, "Feast of Booths"

[7]Literally, "science"

[8]Maître in the original French. This title can also be translated as: "Teacher", or "Rabbi"

[9]*Lithostrotos* from the Greek literally translates as the "pavement." To the North of the Temple esplanade of Jerusalem, where today the Christians commence the Way of the Cross, there are various ruins amongst which the famous arch of the "Ecce Homo" (behold the man), the pavement popularly called the "Lithostrotos", an underground pool and various other minor structures. These ruins are to be found to the North of the Via Dolorosa Road, both in the Franciscan property where the two medieval chapels of Flagellation and Condemnation stand together with the imposing building of the Studium Biblicum Franciscanum and mainly in the adjacent property of the Sisters of Sion.

84

CPSIA information can be obtained at www.ICGtesting.com
Printed in the USA
BVOW081416300912

301676BV00001BA/5/P

9 781894 981996